spot

HORSES

CLYDESDALE HORSES

by Alissa Thielges

AMICUS

horseshoe

plow

Look for these words and pictures as you read.

coat

feathers

What a big horse!
It is a Clydesdale.

Clydesdales are draft horses.
They pull wagons.
They are from Scotland.

See the horseshoe?
It is the size of a dinner plate.
Clydesdale hooves are big.

horseshoe

See the plow?
Clydesdales pull it.
They help farmers in the field.

coat

See the coat?
It has thick fur.
The horse stays warm.

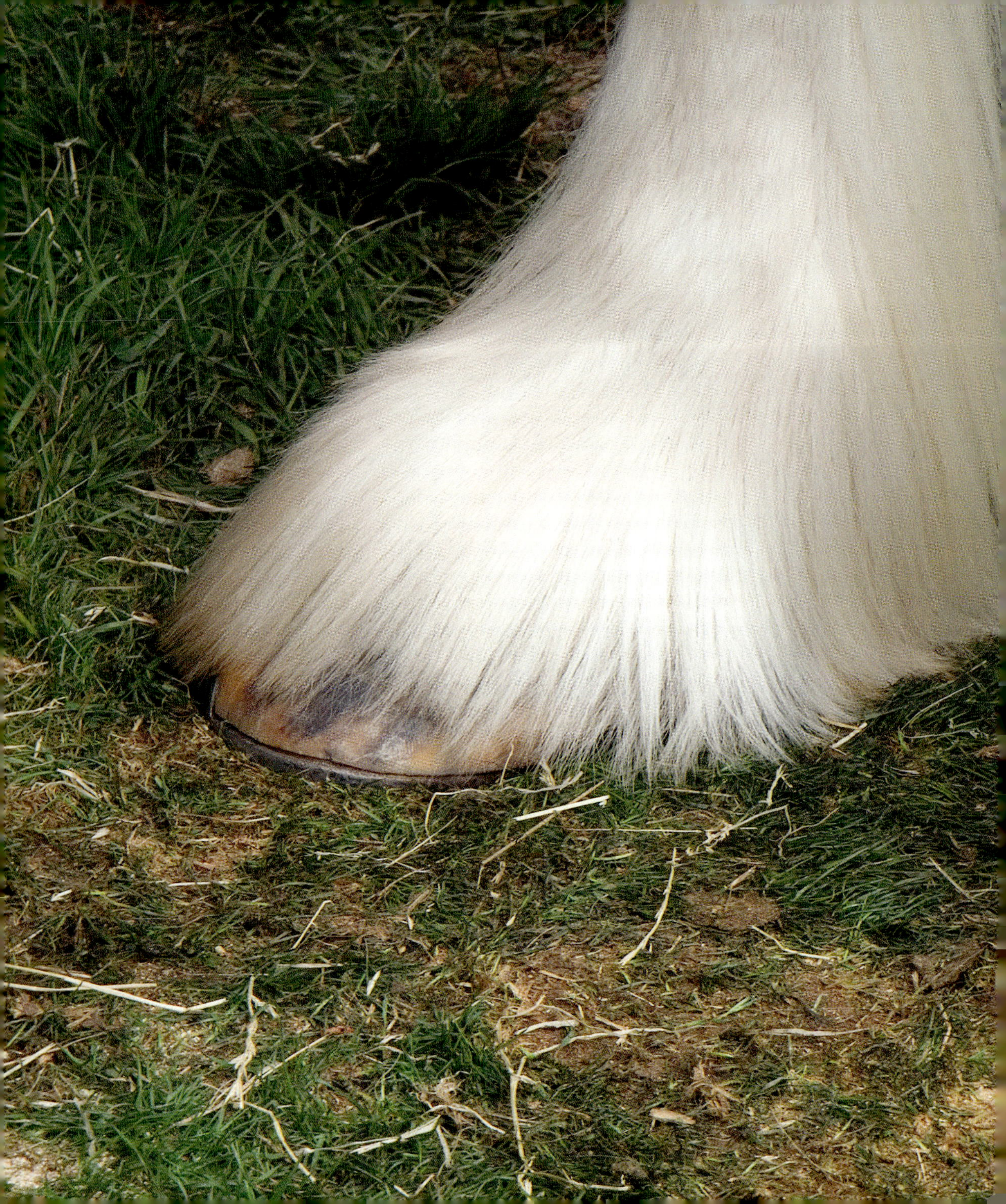

See the feathers?
They are long hairs.
They keep the legs warm.

feathers

The horses pull a sleigh. Giddy up!

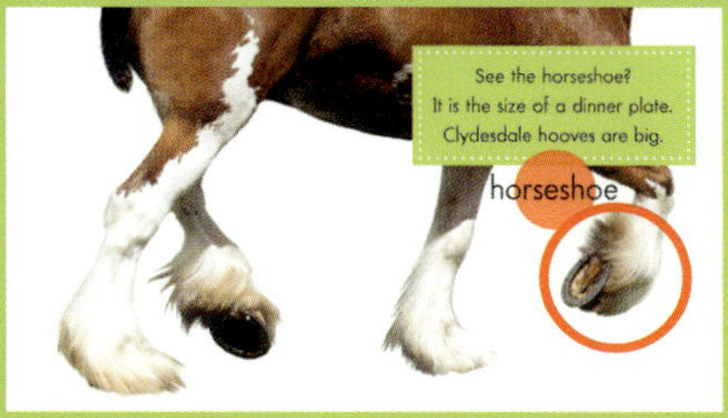

horseshoe

plow

Did you find?

coat

feathers

Spot is published by Amicus
P.O. Box 227, Mankato, MN 56002
www.amicuspublishing.us

Library of Congress Cataloging-in-Publication Data
Names: Thielges, Alissa, 1995- author.
Title: Clydesdale horses / by Alissa Thielges.
Description: Mankato, Minnesota : Amicus, [2023] | Series: Spot horses | Audience: Ages 4-7 | Audience: Grades K-1 | Summary: "Meet the Clydesdale horse breed in this leveled reader that reinforces key vocabulary with a search-and-find feature. Carefully controlled text and excellent photos introduce these large draft horses to early readers."—Provided by publisher.
Identifiers: LCCN 2021055483 (print) | LCCN 2021055484 (ebook) | ISBN 9781645492467 (hardcover) | ISBN 9781681527703 (paperback) | ISBN 9781645493341 (ebook)
Subjects: LCSH: Clydesdale horse--Juvenile literature.
Classification: LCC SF293.C65 T45 2023 (print) | LCC SF293.C65 (ebook) | DDC 636.1/5--dc23/eng/20211213
LC record available at https://lccn.loc.gov/2021055483
LC ebook record available at https://lccn.loc.gov/2021055484

Rebecca Glaser, editor
Deb Miner, series designer
Catherine Berthiaume and Grant Gould, book design and photo research

Photos by Alamy/Juniors Bildarchiv GmbH 3, Bert Hoferichter 4-5, Peter Jordan_NE 12-13, Tamara Gooch 14-15; iStock/Gannet77 6-7; Shutterstock/OlesyaNickolaeva/cover 16, Anastasija Popova 1, OryPhotography 10-11; Wikimedia Commons/Bernard Spragg 8-9